IN FOCUS: NATIVE AMERICANS

BLACKFOOT

HISTORY AND CULTURE

MARK STEWART

Cavendish Square

Published in 2026 by Cavendish Square Publishing, LLC
2544 Clinton Street, Buffalo, NY 14224

Website: cavendishsq.com

Portions of this work were originally authored by Chelly Dwyer and published as *Blackfoot* (Spotlight on Native Americans). All new material in this edition authored by Mark Stewart.

Publisher: Katie Kawa
Book Design: Lisa Miley

Portions of this work were reviewed by: Robert J. Conley, Former Sequoyah Distinguished Professor at Western Carolina University and Director of Native American Studies at Morningside College and Montana State University.

Photo Credits: © Salvatore Vasapolli/Animals Animals/age footstock (4); Paul Kane (5*); Library of Congress (6 top*, 16*, 19 top*, 21*); © Roy Ooms/All Canada Photos/age footstock (6 bottom); © Michelle Gilders/age footstock (7); Mary Evans Picture Library (9); Carmelo Guadagno/ Museum of the American Indian (10*); Karl Bodmer (11*); Charles M. Russell (12*); Library and Archives of Canada (13*, 18*, 29 top*); V.O. Hammon Publishing (14*); Carlisle Indian School Digital Resource Center (15); The Meat Eater (19 bottom); Peter Newark's American Pictures (22); Missoula Art Museum (23); Courtesy of Blood Tribe/Kainaiwa (24); Blackfoot Ace Casinos (25); Eye Ubiquitous/Universal Images Group via Getty Images (26); Defense Visual Information Distribution Service (28); Wolfgang Kaehler/SuperStock (29 bottom).

Cover images (clockwise from top): Native Stock; Eye Ubiquitous/Universal Images Group via Getty Images; Karl Bodmer*; Library of Congress*; Native Stock; Native Stock.

*These images are in the public domain

Cataloging-in-Publication Data
Names: Stewart, Mark, 1960 July 7-.
Title: Blackfoot history and culture / Mark Stewart.
Description: Buffalo, NY : Cavendish Square Publishing, 2026. | Series: In focus: Native Americans | Includes glossary and index.
Identifiers: ISBN 9781502674944 (pbk.) | ISBN 9781502674951 (library bound) | ISBN 9781502674968 (ebook)
Subjects: LCSH: Siksika Indians--Juvenile literature. | Siksika Indians--Social life and customs--Juvenile literature. | Siksika Indians--History--Juvenile literature.
Classification: LCC E99.S54 S94 2026 | DDC 978.004'97352--dc23

CPSIA compliance information: Batch #CS26CSQ: For further information contact Cavendish Square Publishing LLC at 1-877-980-4450.
Printed in the United States of America

CONTENTS

ABOUT OUR GLOSSARY

In this book, there may be several words or terms you are reading for the first time, or words that are familiar but used in an unusual way. All of these words appear in **bold type** throughout the book and are defined on page 30.

I AM THE LAND

The North American **prairie** is a breathtaking sweep of grasslands stretching north from Texas into Canada. It extends from the Great Lakes region west to the Rocky Mountains. Its wide-open spaces, abundance of large game, and hundreds of species of plants have made it an attractive home to humans for more than 10,000 years. The Blackfoot tribe—or Blackfeet, as they are known in the United States—were "newcomers" to this area. We know this because the language they speak, which has roots in the **Algonquian** family, is typical of tribes in Eastern Canada, over 1,500 miles (2,414 km) away. Most historians believe the Blackfeet were the first people from this region to migrate west to the Great Plains.

The Blackfeet eventually settled between the Missouri River in Montana and the Canadian Provinces

This painting from the 1840s shows Big Snake recounting his exploits to five lesser Blackfeet chiefs. Blackfeet warriors were superb fighters.

of Alberta and Saskatchewan—an area east of the Rocky Mountains measuring roughly 400 miles (644 km) from top to bottom. The centuries-long trek from the east was made on foot, using simple, two-poled sleds called travoises. Travoises were typically pulled by dogs and used to transport all of a family's belongings.

As the Blackfeet moved west, they came into contact with other tribes, who defended their territory and resources. Blackfoot warriors became superb fighters,

◀ Chief Mountain is one of the most recognizable natural landmarks on the reservation in Montana.

Fat Horse poses for the camera in the traditional dress of a Blackfoot soldier. This photo was taken in the 1920s.

but they met their match in the early 1700s when they encountered the Shoshone people, who fought on horseback. The stunned Blackfeet called horses "elk dogs."

The Blackfeet were able to obtain horses through their neighbors, who included the Flathead, Kootenai, and Nez Perce people. They formed a close alliance with the Crees, who spoke a similar language and also had roots in Eastern Canada. The Crees were expert trappers who exchanged animal pelts with French fur traders for metal tools and firearms. It was from the Cree and Assiniboine tribes that the Blackfeet obtained guns. The combination of guns and horses made the Blackfeet formidable warriors, particularly against enemies who used traditional weapons, such as bows and arrows.

The Blackfoot people call themselves *niitsitapii*, or "the real people." The tribe's name was invented by the Crees, who called them *Siksikauw*, or "black-footed people," because the bottoms of their moccasins were black. A Blackfoot legend tells the story of a long-ago tribe that split into groups in search of food. When they met later, one group had red faces and hands, because they had been eating berries. They became the Kanai, or Bloods. Another group had journeyed through a burnt patch of prairie. Their footwear and leggings were black.

Like all Great Plains tribes, the Blackfoot people followed the bison herds and depended on the animals for many of their needs.

Today, the Blackfoot tribe is divided into three groups: the Siksika Nation, Kanai Nation, and Peigan Nation, all of whom live in Canada. The Southern Piegan, who call themselves Blackfeet, live in Montana on the Canadian border. The spelling of Peigan/ Piegan differs in Canada and the United States.

FIRST CONTACT

Because they moved constantly north and west, the Blackfeet rarely came into contact with Europeans during the 1700s. Occasionally, they traded furs, bison robes, and dried meat with French trappers and British forts in Canada. The benefit of limited contact was that it helped the Blackfeet avoid the diseases that ravaged many other tribes. In fact, they were more likely to contract a serious illness from neighboring tribes, like the Crees, who had regular **interaction** with Europeans.

World events eventually brought the Blackfoot people in closer contact. In 1800, French dictator Napoleon Bonaparte made a treaty with Spain that gave France control of much of the land west of the Mississippi River. In 1803, Napoleon sold this land to the United States. President Thomas Jefferson tasked Meriwether Lewis and William Clark to lead an expedition to explore America's new territory. When they reached the **headwaters** of the Missouri River, they came into contact with the Blackfeet.

The arrival of miners and other fortune seekers on tribal land led to the signing of treaties beginning in the 1850s.

Over the next half-century, more and more Americans poured through the tribe's territory on their way to the West Coast, where gold and rich farmland awaited. In 1855, Blackfoot leaders signed a treaty with the U.S. government promising to allow settlers to pass through their land safely, and to allow railroads and telegraph lines to be constructed across their territory. In exchange, the tribe received a large reservation in northwest Montana, along with annual payments and training to become ranchers. Blackfoot bands in Canada would soon come under similar pressure.

I AM A WARRIOR

Boys in the Blackfoot culture were raised to be hunters and warriors. Their early training involved guarding horses, reading animal tracks, and learning how to use a bow and arrow. When a boy killed his first animal, the family held a feast to celebrate. Later, boys were taught hand-to-hand combat. By the time they were ready to face an enemy, Blackfoot warriors were skilled in the use of tomahawks. They were also expected to fight to the death.

The Blackfoot warrior tradition developed over many centuries, dating back to the tribe's time in Eastern Canada. During the journey to the Great Plains, they would have encountered hostile tribes at almost

This museum display shows the tools, weapons, and clothing a Blackfoot warrior had at his disposal. Many artifacts like these are now being returned to tribal ownership.

Mounted Blackfoot warriors were extremely successful in battle. They had great skill and endurance.

every stop. The skills to attack and defend were a matter of survival. Blackfoot warriors were known for their strength and **endurance**, which helped them outlast enemies and win long battles.

Even before they acquired horses and firearms, Blackfoot warriors were among the most ferocious fighters on the Great Plains. Once they possessed these new weapons of war, they became an awesome military power. Their horsemanship was greatly admired, as were their battle tactics. They specialized in disorienting their enemies with lightning attacks, ambushes, and false retreats.

As the Blackfeet spread throughout the region, they pushed other tribes in front of them—some entirely through the Rockies to land on the other side of the mountains. They also protected their hunting grounds

Blackfoot battle tactics included close combat, as well as surprise and deception.

from **poachers**, including American, British, and French fur traders in search of valuable beaver pelts.

With American and Canadian settlers streaming into their lands, the Blackfoot tribes made treaties to ensure their survival. However, not all Blackfeet supported these agreements. Attacks on settlers between 1865 and 1870 came to be known as the Blackfoot Wars, and brought them into conflict with the U.S. Army. The violence impacted everyone. In 1870, the army mistakenly attacked the camp of Chief Heavy Runner, who was not responsible for any of the raids. Soldiers killed about 200 innocent people in what became known as the Marias River Massacre.

In 1870, Cree and Assiniboine warriors launched a large-scale raid on a Blackfoot band in Alberta, Canada, believing the tribe had been badly weakened by a **smallpox** epidemic. However, a group of warriors from Blood and Peigan camps rushed to repel the raiders and demonstrated their skill and bravery by killing nearly 300 attackers. The Battle of the Belly River was the last major battle between Native tribes in North America. Chief Big Bear (left) led Cree forces in the conflict.

A NEW REALITY

In 1870, the Hudson Bay Company, which owned the land in Western Canada, sold Blackfoot territory to the Canadian government. Canada, which was a British province at the time, then made a treaty with the tribe. It exchanged 50,000 square miles (129,500 sq km) of Blackfoot territory for reservation land and annual payments. Most of the people continued to hunt rather than switch to farming and ranching. However, by 1880, the bison herds on which the Blackfeet relied had been hunted out.

In Canada and the United States, the adjustment to life on reservations was difficult. Many perished during the winter of 1883–84.

With their traditional food supply gone, the Blackfoot people faced a grim **transition** to

A group of Piegan chiefs pose for a photo in 1891. They were visiting the Carlisle Indian School in Pennsylvania, a government boarding school that forced Native American children to assimilate into white society.

reservation life. During the winter of 1883–84, one-quarter of the Southern Peigan tribe starved to death. In the decades that followed, the tribe transitioned to farming and ranching, but were always dependent on food and supplies from the U.S. and Canadian governments.

Improvements came slowly. The Canadian government began providing more agricultural support and social services following World War II. During the 1970s, Canada funded modern housing and electricity on the reservations. Following a 1964 flood, the U.S. government sent money to build houses, roads, and dams on Blackfoot lands in Montana.

BEING BLACKFOOT

Like all **nomadic** people, the Blackfoot tribe moved with the seasons to take advantage of the resources available in the forests, mountains, and open plains. The tribe divided into **self-sufficient** bands that lived together throughout the winter in tipis (tepees) that were set up in wooded river valleys. Bands usually numbered between 100 and 200 people, and were typically made up of extended family groups, with an agreed-upon leader. This person was almost always a warrior who had proved his bravery, but who also was respected for his judgment, wisdom, and generosity. Bands identified themselves with names that recalled an event or described band members, like the Many Fat Horses band and the All Short People band.

During the long winter months, Blackfoot bands hunted and trapped game. They also ate preserved meat, roots, and pemmican. Spring was a time for repairs of tipis, riding equipment, clothing, and anything else that

As Blackfoot families moved with the seasons, they used a simple, framed structure called a travois to transport their belongings.

wore out during the winter. In June, Blackfoot bands came together to begin hunting bison, which provided meat, hides, and warm clothing. One bison weighed between 1,500 and 2,000 pounds (680 to 907 kg) and Blackfoot villages used every part of the animal. In a good year, there might be a surplus of food and skins that could be traded.

The entire tribe moved through the summer and fall, following the bison herds and catching trout in the rivers that cut through their territory. While the men were occupied with hunting and fishing, Blackfoot women harvested local plants, dried bison meat, and began making pemmican for when the bands returned to their winter camps. Women owned the tipis, which they decorated with fantastic designs and images.

Blackfoot medicine women were critical to the survival of a band. Among their duties was to assist mothers in safely delivering their children. Babies were

washed and painted red. Their umbilical cords were cut with an arrowhead and preserved in beaded containers shaped like a snake (for boys) or a lizard (for girls). The tribe believed that these animals lived long lives and never became ill—a future they wished for their children. Boys and girls played together until around the age of five, after which they began learning adult skills. Women were also caretakers of the sacred bundles. A sacred bundle was a group of objects tied in a cloth or hide package that was used for religious ceremonies.

This painting shows a typical summer encampment, which brought together many Blackfoot bands.

Pemmican was a mixture of dried meat, animal fat, and berries that Indigenous people in North America had been making for thousands of years.

In Blackfoot society, women owned the family tipi.

SOMETHING SACRED

Origin stories are an important part of Blackfoot culture. Apistotoke is one of several names for the Great Spirit, creator of all things—including the sky, sun, moon, stars, and the earth itself. Apistotoke also created Na'pi, the first human, who then created the rest of humankind. Blackfoot myths also account for many aspects of the natural world, such as the seasons. Na'pi is said to have found bags containing summer and winter, and through a series of events, also created the wind. It was so strong that it nearly carried him off a mountaintop, but he held tight to a birch tree. This accounts for the markings on its bark.

In another story, Na'pi made water of different colors and gave it to people to drink. Each color corresponded to a different language. The people who received the black water all spoke the Blackfoot language. Blackfoot culture and tradition is preserved through the telling of these stories, as is the language

The effort to capture Blackfoot origin stories and preserve the language dates back more than a century. Here Chief Mountain speaks into an early recording device.

itself. It is taught to every child who attends school on their reservations.

Art also holds an important place in the Blackfoot culture. It is perhaps no surprise that a people who traveled more than halfway across the North American continent would be known for their footwear. Not only is the tribe named for the color of its moccasins, it has focused much of its creativity on them. Originally decorated with geometric patterns made with porcupine quills, Blackfoot moccasins went to the next level after the tribe began trading for glass beads in the 1700s. Today's Blackfoot artists bead moccasins using traditional symbols and patterns, including flowers, but they also borrow designs from other Native American tribes in their work. These **intricately** designed moccasins are worn in ceremonies and are highly prized by collectors around the world.

The Blackfoot artistic tradition extends to the performing arts and the written word. David John Dragonfly, a Blackfoot-Assiniboine artist, celebrates

Among the most important Blackfoot spiritual celebrations and ceremonies was the Sun Dance, which took place over several days. It was a test of endurance and sacrifice, during which a warrior was attached to a central pole through piercings in his chest. Friends and families gathered around the dancers to support and pray for them. Many North American tribes held Sun Dance ceremonies, with each reflecting an individual aspect of its culture. For many years, the U.S. and Canadian governments outlawed the Sun Dance, claiming it was too dangerous and violent. In truth, this was part of a greater plan to extinguish tribal culture and tradition.

the breathtaking beauty of the tribe's Montana reservation. He is inspired by the **pictographic** art of the Great Plains tribes and his work has been featured at the National Museum of the American Indian in Washington, D.C.

▲ Stephen Graham Jones draws on Native American themes to produce popular science fiction books.

Beverly Hungry Wolf, who grew up on the Blood reservation in Canada, has written several books about the Blackfoot people, including stories collected from women who grew up on reservations in the early 1900s—and who attended the boarding schools where many Blackfoot children were sent.

Stephen Graham Jones, a member of the Blackfeet tribe in Montana, has become one of the most popular fantasy and horror authors of the 21st century. His novels and short stories feature strange characters and dark humor. He has won the Bram Stoker Award for fantasy writing several times. *The Only Good Indians*, a horror story published in 2020, won the prestigious Ray Bradbury Prize for Science Fiction.

PAST, PRESENT, FUTURE

The Blackfoot Confederacy represents the four Blackfoot reservations (in Canada they are called *reserves*) in North America. Although each has its own government and head chief, members come together several times a year for cultural, religious, and social events. That can get complicated sometimes. For example, in 2002, Canadian Kainai Chief Chris Shade was not allowed to bring his eagle-feather warbonnet into the United States for a confederacy meeting. In the Unites States, Native Americans must have a permit to possess eagle feathers because eagles are a protected species. Eagles are protected in

Ceremonial headdresses like this one can be difficult to pass through customs because of different regulations in Canada and the United States.

This is a poker chip from the Ace Blackfoot Casino in Calgary, Canada.

Canada, too, but the country does not have the same permit requirement. So the headdress had to stay north of the border.

Chief Shade was on his way to a gathering at the Blackfeet Indian Reservation of Montana. More than 10,000 people live on the reservation, which is located on the eastern edge of Glacier National Park, a popular tourism destination in the northwest part of the state. Nearly as many tribal members live elsewhere. The Blackfeet operate many businesses that cater to park visitors, including a resort and casino, guided tours, and the Museum of the Plains Indians. The local economy

also includes cattle farming and oil and gas **leases** on tribal land. The tribe's headquarters is in Browning, which plays host to North American Indian Days every summer.

The Kainai (Blood) reserve is the largest in Canada, covering 545 square miles (1,412 sq km). More than 4,500 people live on the reserve, with another 8,000 tribal members living elsewhere. In addition to successful farming operations, the reserve is a source of Ammolite, a rare **organic gemstone** that is highly prized in Asia. The Piikani (Peigan) reserve has around 4,000 tribal members. The Siksika (Northern Blackfoot) reserve is home to more than 4,000 tribal members, with 3,400 more living elsewhere.

The Blackfoot Confederacy addresses border difficulties, brings jobs and government funding to the tribes, and works with museums to return tribal treasures. In 2024, a rare women's headdress was **repatriated** and is now in possession of the Siksika people for the first time in over a century. The artifact is made of bison horns, sacred bird feathers, and porcupine quills, and is adorned with

◀ A member of the Montana Blackfeet tribe participates in a dance competition in Alberta, Canada.

Artifacts belonging to Chief Crowfoot are among the Blackfoot items being returned to tribal possession.

red cloth and brass bells. It had been housed at the Royal Albert Memorial Museum and Art Gallery in England. Two years earlier, the same museum returned a collection of clothing and artifacts belonging to Chief Crowfoot, a famous Siksika leader from the 1800s. They are now on display at Blackfoot Crossing Historical Park in Alberta.

Canada's Peigan reserve is home to a "buffalo jump" used by Indigenous people to drive bison from a favorite grazing area off a 36-foot (11 m) cliff. The Head-Smashed-In Buffalo Jump is a UNESCO World Heritage Site.

Lucy Threefingers of the Blackfeet tribe of Montana performs the traditional Fancy Shawl Dance during American Indian Heritage Month. Performances like this help to preserve tribal traditions.

GLOSSARY AND FURTHER READING

GLOSSARY

Algonquian—A family of Indigenous languages originating from the Atlantic and Great Lakes regions.

Endurance—The ability to do something difficult for a long time.

Headwaters—The shallow streams that are the source of rivers.

Interaction—Direct involvement with others.

Intricately—In a detailed way.

Leases—Agreements that give certain rights to others in exchange for payment.

Nomadic—Moving from place to place.

Organic Gemstones—Rare stones formed from living things instead of minerals, such as pearls.

Pictographic—Using symbols instead of letters to convey an idea.

Poachers—People who catch fish and game without permission.

Prairie—A large open grassland.

Repatriated—Sent back to its original country.

Self-Sufficient—Needing no outside help.

Smallpox—A virus brought to the Americas by Europeans, for which Indigenous people had no natural immunity. By the mid-1800s, more than 75 percent of Native Americans may have died of the disease.

Transition—The process of changing from one condition to another.

BOOKS

Krupat, Arnold. *Boarding School Voices: Carlisle Indian School Students Speak*. Lincoln, NE: University of Nebraska Press, 2021.

Rossiter, Brienna. *The Trail of Tears*. Mendota Heights, MN: North Star Editions, 2025.

Tyler, Ron. *Native Americans: The Complete Plates of McKenney, Catlin, and Bodmer*. Cologne, Germany: Taschen America, 2024.

Various Authors. *My Life: Growing Up Native in America*. New York, NY: MTV Books/Simon & Schuster Children's Publishing, 2024.

ABOUT THE AUTHOR

MARK STEWART has written more than 150 nonfiction books for educational publishers, covering history, sports, and popular culture. His family tree tells a complex story common to many Americans. Mark's ancestors include some of the first European colonists, as well as the Indigenous people with whom early settlers interacted. Some faced off on the field of battle while others fought side-by-side. His 10th great-grandfather was **Myles Standish**, an officer on the ***Mayflower***, while his ninth great-grandmother was **Singing Bird Corbison**, who was described as a "Shawnee woman" but who was probably from the **Wampanoag** tribe. The Wampanoag people saved Standish and his fellow **Pilgrims** from starvation during the winter of 1620–21, forming the basis for the story of Thanksgiving. The descendants of Corbison and Standish blended into a single family in 1789, and then headed west in search of opportunity. This brought Mark's ancestors into direct conflict with Native people along the frontier in the 1700s and 1800s. Mark's sixth great-grandmother recalled frantically casting bullets for her husband as they defended their small Kentucky fort from an attack. Another served under 23-year-old **Abraham Lincoln** in the Illinois Militia during the Black Hawk War of 1832. Mark's more recent ancestors chose to fight their battles with words—as writers and editors of books, newspapers and magazines. In 2007, he authored a history of the **Indian Removal Act of 1830** and the infamous **Trail of Tears**.

INDEX